W9-AXA-989

Let's Discover Canada
ALBERTA

by
Suzanne LeVert

George Sheppard
McMaster University
General Editor

CHELSEA HOUSE PUBLISHERS
New York   Philadelphia

Cover: Pump jacks dot hayfields in oil-rich southern Alberta.
Opposite: A skier competes at the 1988 Winter Olympics in Calgary.

Chelsea House Publishers
EDITOR-IN-CHIEF: Remmel Nunn
MANAGING EDITOR: Karyn Gullen Browne
COPY CHIEF: Juliann Barbato
PICTURE EDITOR: Adrian G. Allen
ART DIRECTOR: Maria Epes
DEPUTY COPY CHIEF: Mark Rifkin
ASSISTANT ART DIRECTOR: Noreen Romano
MANUFACTURING MANAGER: Gerald Levine
SYSTEMS MANAGER: Lindsey Ottman
PRODUCTION MANAGER: Joseph Romano
PRODUCTION COORDINATOR: Marie Claire Cebrián

Let's Discover Canada
SENIOR EDITOR: Rebecca Stefoff

Staff for ALBERTA
COPY EDITOR: Benson D. Simmonds
EDITORIAL ASSISTANT: Ian Wilker
PICTURE RESEARCH: Joan Beard
DESIGNER: Diana Blume

First Printing

1 3 5 7 9 8 6 4 2

Library of Congress Cataloging-in-Publication Data
LeVert, Suzanne.
    Let's discover Canada. Alberta/by Suzanne LeVert;
George Sheppard, general editor.
        p.   cm.
    Includes bibliographical references and index.
    Summary: Discusses the geography, history, and culture of the
Canadian province of Alberta.
    ISBN 0-7910-1026-0
    1. Alberta—Juvenile literature. [1. Alberta.] I. Sheppard,
George C. B. II. Title.
F1076.4.L48   1991
971.23—dc20

90-46037
CIP
AC

Contents

My Canada

by Pierre Berton

"Nobody knows my country," a great Canadian journalist, Bruce Hutchison, wrote almost half a century ago. It is still true. Most Americans, I think, see Canada as a pleasant vacationland and not much more. And yet we are the United States's greatest single commercial customer, and the United States is our largest customer.

Lacking a major movie industry, we have made no wide-screen epics to chronicle our triumphs and our tragedies. But then there has been little blood in our colonial past—no revolutions, no civil war, not even a wild west. Yet our history is crammed with remarkable men and women. I am thinking of Joshua Slocum, the first man to sail alone around the world, and Robert Henderson, the prospector who helped start the Klondike gold rush. I am thinking of some of our famous artists and writers—comedian Dan Aykroyd, novelists Margaret Atwood and Robertson Davies, such popular performers as Michael J. Fox, Anne Murray, Gordon Lightfoot, and k.d. lang, and hockey greats from Maurice Richard to Gordie Howe to Wayne Gretzky.

The real shape of Canada explains why our greatest epic has been the building of the Pacific Railway to unite the nation from

sea to sea in 1885. On the map, the country looks square. But because the overwhelming majority of Canadians live within 100 miles (160 kilometers) of the U.S. border, in practical terms the nation is long and skinny. We are in fact an archipelago of population islands separated by implacable barriers—the angry ocean, three mountain walls, and the Canadian Shield, that vast desert of billion-year-old rock that sprawls over half the country, rich in mineral treasures, impossible for agriculture.

Canada's geography makes the country difficult to govern and explains our obsession with transportation and communication. The government has to be as involved in railways, airlines, and broadcasting networks as it is with social services such as universal medical care. Rugged individualism is not a Canadian quality. Given the environment, people long ago learned to work together for security.

It is ironic that the very bulwarks that separate us—the chiseled peaks of the Selkirk Mountains, the gnarled scarps north of Lake Superior, the ice-choked waters of the Northumberland Strait —should also be among our greatest attractions for tourists and artists. But if that is the paradox of Canada, it is also the glory.

Rising from the prairie is Edmonton, the capital of Alberta and an important center of business and transportation in Canada's West.

CANADA

UNITED STATES

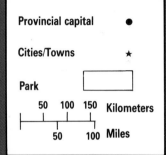

Provincial capital   ●

Cities/Towns   ★

Park

50   100   150   **Kilometers**

50   100   **Miles**

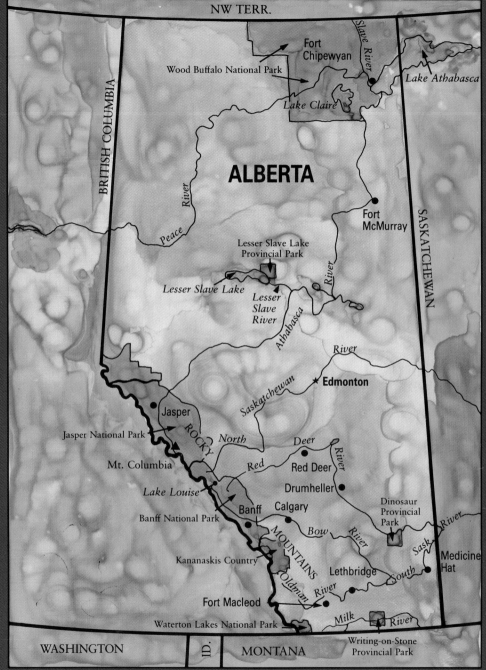

NW TERR.

BRITISH COLUMBIA

Fort Chipewyan

Wood Buffalo National Park

Slave River

Lake Athabasca

Lake Claire

ALBERTA

SASKATCHEWAN

Fort McMurray

Peace River

Lesser Slave Lake Provincial Park

Lesser Slave Lake

Lesser Slave River

Athabasca River

River

Edmonton

Saskatchewan River

Jasper

Jasper National Park

ROCKY

North

Mt. Columbia

Red

Deer

Red Deer

River

Lake Louise

Drumheller

Banff

Calgary

Dinosaur Provincial Park

Banff National Park

MOUNTAINS

Bow

River

Sask. River

Kananaskis Country

Lethbridge

South

Medicine Hat

Oldman River

Fort Macleod

Milk

River

Waterton Lakes National Park

Writing-on-Stone Provincial Park

WASHINGTON

ID.

MONTANA

Wild rose

Great horned owl

Shield of arms

Alberta at a Glance

Area: 255,285 square miles (661,185 square kilometers)
Population: 2,365,825 (1986 census)
Capital: Edmonton (population 574,000)
Other cities: Calgary (pop. 636,100), Lethbridge (pop. 59,000), Red Deer (pop. 52,000), Medicine Hat (pop. 42,000)
Major rivers: Peace, Slave, Athabasca, North Saskatchewan, South Saskatchewan, Red Deer
Major lakes: Lesser Slave, Claire, Athabasca
Highest point: Mt. Columbia, 12,294 feet (3,725 meters)
Principal products: Petroleum, natural gas, coal, wheat, barley, livestock
Entered Dominion of Canada: September 1, 1905

Motto: *Fortis et liber* ("Strong and free")
Provincial flower: Wild rose (also called prickly rose)
Provincial tree: Lodgepole pine
Provincial bird: Great horned owl
Government: Parliamentary system with a single-chambered legislature of 79 members, who are elected to 5-year terms by the people in their district; the formal head of state is the lieutenant governor, who is appointed by the federal government in Ottawa as the representative of the Crown; the head of government is the premier; the premier and executive council are members of the legislature; Alberta is represented in the federal government in Ottawa by 6 senators and 21 members of the House of Commons

The Land

Alberta has an abundance of natural resources, including some of North America's largest reserves of oil and natural gas. Sometimes called the Sunshine Province, Alberta is also known for clear blue skies, a temperate climate, and spectacular landscapes that include huge lakes, surging rivers, sweeping plains, and jagged ice-capped mountains.

With an area of 255,285 square miles (661,185 square kilometers), Alberta is the fourth largest province in Canada, after Quebec, Ontario, and British Columbia. It is bordered on the west by British Columbia, on the north by the Northwest Territories, on the east by Saskatchewan, and on the south by the U.S. state of Montana. Alberta is the westernmost of Canada's three prairie provinces; the others are Manitoba and Saskatchewan. About three-fourths of Alberta is part of the North American High Plains, a wide belt of grassland that covers much of central Canada and the central United States. Of the three prairie provinces, Alberta has the most diverse landscape. It is the only province that contains all three of Canada's major geographic formations. The rocky barrens in the far northeast are part of the

Opposite: Nestled in a Rocky Mountain valley is the Banff Springs Hotel, built to resemble a Scottish castle. The hotel and the town of Banff are located in Banff National Park, which was Canada's first national park.
Above: Red Rock Canyon is part of Waterton Lakes, a national park on Alberta's southern border that adjoins Glacier National Park in Montana. The vivid color is caused by iron deposits in the rock.

Canadian Shield, the ancient bedrock of North America; the center of the province is part of the High Plains; and the high ranges on the province's southwestern border are part of the Rocky Mountains.

Geographic Regions and Wildlife

Alberta's geography was shaped by the passage of the glaciers during the last ice age, which ended about 10,000 years ago. The ice sheets gouged valleys, carved hills and mountains, and formed the beds of rivers and lakes. Although the glaciers retreated from the lowlands many thousands of years ago, remnants of them are found among the high mountain peaks. The 150-square-mile (389-square-kilometer) Columbia Icefield is a reminder of an age when the entire province was covered by a thick blanket of ice and snow.

Today, Alberta is a mixture of mountainous wilderness, hilly grassland, and a semiarid area that is almost a desert. The north is a vast evergreen forest of spruce, balsam fir, and tamarack, dotted with sparkling lakes and powerful rivers—except for the Peace River valley, which has broad, fertile plains and is one of the northernmost areas of productive farmland in the world. The wildlife of the region includes moose, mule deer, woodland caribou, black bears, timber wolves, lynx, beavers, muskrat, otters, and foxes. The most dramatic wild inhabitant of the north, however, is the bison, or wood buffalo. These high-shouldered, shaggy beasts once roamed over most of Alberta. They are now found largely in Wood Buffalo National Park.

A prairie landscape prevails in the south-central interior of the province. Groves of aspen dot the grasslands; coyotes, gophers, jackrabbits, badgers, grouse, and ducks are numerous. The plains of this region consist of dark, clayey soil. The clay holds water well and absorbs many nutrients and minerals that are vital for plant growth, so the area offers excellent pastureland and farmland. But Alberta's plains are known for more than their agricultural productivity. Beneath the fertile soil lie vast deposits of oil, coal, and natural gas. These give the province its chief economic resource—energy.

Coal and oil are called fossil fuels because they are derived from the remnants of plants that lived and died millions of years ago. Alberta is rich in other types of fossils as well. Some of the most complete dinosaur remains in the world have been discovered in the province. Most of the fossil fields are located in the southern part of the province, in the stretches of semiarid territory that are called badlands because of their stark, inhospitable landscapes. The badlands are dry and bleak, with sparse, desertlike vegetation such as hardy grasses and shrubs. Centuries of wind and rain have eroded the rocky hills and gullies of the badlands, exposing fossils that were buried there eons ago. Erosion has also created the strange and striking rock formations called hoodoos. These are toadstool-shaped rocks—some as big as houses—that seem to grow out of the sandstone cliffs of the

Wood buffalo were once found throughout the forests of northern Alberta. They have become rare, and most of them live in parks and preserves.

The badlands of southern Alberta contain hoodoos—sandstone formations carved by wind and water over thousands of years. These hoodoos are near the city of Drumheller.

badlands because their bases have been eroded to slender stalks. The badlands and the hoodoos are among the most popular tourist attractions in Alberta.

The rugged, towering Rocky Mountains form Alberta's southwestern border with the province of British Columbia. Some of Canada's most magnificent scenery is found in this area. To preserve the region's natural beauty, a string of national and provincial parks has been established along the spine of the mountains. The biggest of these are Jasper National Park and Banff National Park. Many peaks between 8,000 and 11,000 feet (2,400 and 3,300 meters) in altitude are found in Alberta's Canadian Rockies. The tallest is Mount Columbia, which rises to 12,294 feet (3,747 meters) and is situated on the provincial border in Jasper National Park. Several life zones exist in the Rockies. Above the tree line, at heights greater than about 7,000 feet (2,100 meters), is the cold, windy alpine zone. Here mountain goats and bighorn sheep forage among moss-covered boulders. Farther down is the subalpine zone, where spruce, fir, and other evergreens thrive and grizzly bears and mountain caribou are found. The lowest slopes and valley bottoms are in the temperate zone. Trees in this zone include cottonwood, birch, poplar, spruce, larch, and lodgepole pine; wildlife includes eagles, beavers, squirrels, moose, and bears.

Rivers and Lakes

Rivers and lakes cover 6,485 square miles (16,796 square kilometers) of the province; this is about 2 percent of Canada's total freshwater resources. About 80 percent of Alberta's fresh water is found in its northern half. The more heavily populated, intensively farmed southern half of the province has only 20 percent of its water.

The rivers of northern Alberta drain into the Mackenzie River drainage system in the Northwest Territories, and they eventually flow into the Arctic Ocean. One of these rivers is the Athabasca, which flows into Lake Athabasca on the border between Alberta and Saskatchewan. Like the Athabasca, the Peace River flows across almost all of the province from west to east. Near the eastern border, the Peace joins the Slave River, an outlet from Lake Athabasca that flows north into Great Slave Lake in

The Athabasca River is fed by glacial meltwater from high in the Rockies. North of Jasper, the river plunges over the Athabasca Falls, with Mt. Kerkeslin in the background.

the Northwest Territories. Lesser Slave Lake, which despite its name is fairly large, is found in north-central Alberta. The province's best-known lake, however, is Lake Louise, a small but scenic lake in Banff National Park in the Rockies. Surrounded by snowcapped peaks and tree-clad slopes, Lake Louise is thought by many to be the most beautiful spot in Canada and is the site of several internationally renowned resorts.

Nearly three-fourths of the water that reaches the southern prairies is carried by two rivers, the North Saskatchewan, which flows through the capital city of Edmonton, and the South Saskatchewan, which is formed by the junction of the Bow and Oldman rivers. The other major river of south-central Alberta is the Red Deer, which flows through some of the most rugged badlands country and joins the South Saskatchewan at the eastern border of the province. Low annual precipitation, high evaporation levels, and fast runoff have created a water shortage in southern Alberta. Irrigation researchers are studying ways to divert some of northern Alberta's abundant water supply to the often parched south.

Climate and Weather

Alberta owes its reputation as Canada's sunniest province to the Rocky Mountains. The mighty mountain range intercepts moist air moving in from the Pacific Ocean and holds back clouds, allowing the sun to shine upon Alberta for about 2,300 hours of each year in the south and 1,800 hours in the north. But sunshine does not guarantee warmth. Although summer brings a few very hot days, most summer weather is relatively cool; July temperatures average about 70 degrees Fahrenheit (21 degrees Centigrade) in the south and about 60°F (16°C) in the north.

Summer is longest in the south. The city of Lethbridge, for example, has a frost-free season of about 111 days, whereas in the northern half of the province the frost-free season shrinks to about 65 days. Albertans then shiver through long, cold winters, with average minimum temperatures ranging from -16°F (-27°C) in the north to 10°F (-12°C) at the southern border. During the

winter, the chinooks give the province occasional breaks from the winter chill. These are warm winter winds that blow from the west and can raise temperatures by as much as 60°F (16°C) in a few hours.

The nearby Rockies affect rainfall and snowfall in Alberta. The mountainous regions may receive more than 20 inches (50 centimeters) of rain a year, whereas the eastern interior plains receive 14 inches (35 centimeters) or fewer, with the southeast being the driest part of the province. About 70 percent of all precipitation in the province falls from May to October. The remaining 30 percent falls during the winter, in the form of snow.

Agriculture is big business in Alberta, especially on the prairies and along the Peace River. Oats, barley, and wheat are the major crops.

The History

Long before European explorers glimpsed what is now Alberta, Native American civilizations existed there. Archaeologists have identified more than 10,000 sites of prehistoric dwellings and activities in the province. Some important Native American relics are found along a river in southern Alberta's Writing-on-Stone Provincial Park. Here petroglyphs that may have had religious or magical meanings were carved into sandstone cliffs long ago. The province is also dotted with buffalo jumps, sites where Native hunters stampeded herds of buffalo over cliffs. The largest of these is the Head-Smashed-In jump, located near Fort Macleod in the southwest. It was used from about 3600 B.C. until the 1880s.

When the first Europeans arrived in Alberta in the 18th century, about 8,000 Natives lived in the area. Those in the north belonged to the Beaver, the Slave, and the Sarcee tribes. They lived by hunting in the game-filled forests and fishing in the lakes and rivers. Southern Alberta was inhabited by the Blackfoot, the Blood, the Piegan, and the Gros Ventre. These tribes depended on

Opposite: Samson, a Cree chief, was one of the Native leaders who signed treaties with the Europeans in the 19th century. Claiming that those treaties were unjust, many Natives today are struggling for land rights and political participation.
Above: A migrating Blackfoot family carries its possessions on travois, nets slung between poles and drawn by horses. This photo was taken in southern Alberta in 1885.

the buffalo, eating its meat and using its hide, horns, bones, and tendons for clothing, housing, and weapons. Central Alberta was home to some Cree, although this Native American group lived mostly in present-day Manitoba and Saskatchewan.

Europeans first explored and settled in eastern Canada. As they worked their way west, their influence was felt by the Natives in dramatic ways. Even before the whites reached Alberta, their guns arrived, having been traded for furs by the Europeans in the east and then passed westward among the Natives. At the same time, the horse made its way north after being brought to Mexico by the Spanish. Firearms and horses changed life forever for the Native Americans. Battles between tribes over territory and resources became more deadly, and the use of guns, instead of spears and stampedes, in the buffalo hunt quickly began to deplete the herds.

A regrettable contribution from the Europeans was disease. Smallpox, diphtheria, and measles spread like wildfire soon after the whites arrived because Native Americans had not built up immunities to these common European illnesses. Many tribes were decimated by outbreaks of disease.

The Fur Traders

The first European to visit Alberta was probably Anthony Henday, an agent of the powerful Hudson's Bay Company, a British fur-trading firm that operated in eastern Canada. In 1754, Henday entered present-day Alberta accompanied by a band of Cree. He discovered that his company was not the only one operating in the interior. The Cree were also trading furs with at least two French posts. As it turned out, however, the French did not pose much of a challenge to the Hudson's Bay Company in western Canada. French traders and trappers retreated from the territory during the Seven Years' War between France and England in the late 1750s. Nevertheless, the Hudson's Bay Company did not hold its monopoly on the fur trade for long. A Scottish firm called the North West Company soon began trading, mapping, and settling in the vast Canadian west.

The Scotsman Alexander Mackenzie (1764–1820) was one of the foremost explorers of northern and western Canada. In two epic journeys that started at Fort Chipewyan in Alberta, he reached the Arctic and Pacific oceans.

During the late 18th and early 19th centuries, the two companies sent competing explorers into northern and central Alberta. They also built rival trading posts. The first permanent white residence in the territory was established in 1778 by Peter Pond of the North West Company. Ten years later, Fort Chipewyan was built on the shore of Lake Athabasca to serve as the jumping-off point for the explorations of Alexander Mackenzie, another Northwester. Mackenzie journeyed north along the Slave River and eventually reached the Arctic Ocean, returning to Fort Chipewyan after a trip of 120 days and 2,990 miles (4,812 kilometers). During this trip he explored the

Mackenzie River, a mighty waterway of the Northwest Territories that was named for him. A few years later Mackenzie went west along the Peace River and crossed the Rocky Mountains into what is now British Columbia.

Peter Fidler explored on behalf of the Hudson's Bay Company. He mapped Lake Athabasca and the South Saskatchewan River. His exploits, however, were overshadowed by those of his contemporary, David Thompson, an explorer who worked for both companies. One of Thompson's accomplishments was to make a thorough map of all the fur-trading territories east of the Rocky Mountains.

Along with the explorers came the traders, who set up posts along the rivers and in the forests. When the North West Company became part of the Hudson's Bay Company in 1821, the huge British conglomerate that resulted from the merger controlled northern and western Canada. At this time, all territory west of Ontario was known as Prince Rupert's Land. It consisted of the present-day provinces of Manitoba, Saskatchewan, and Alberta, and most of what is now the Northwest Territories.

Settlement of Prince Rupert's Land was slow. Apart from the fur traders, the only Europeans who came to Alberta in the mid-

The North West Company and the Hudson's Bay Company vied fiercely for control of the valuable fur trade in Canada. This token, issued by the North West Company in exchange for furs, could be traded for goods at the company's stores. It features the beaver, whose pelt was made into waterproof hats and coats that were eagerly sought by Europeans.

1800s were missionaries in search of Native Americans to convert to Christianity. A Methodist minister named Robert Rundle became the province's first resident clergyman in 1840. Two years later he was followed by a Roman Catholic priest named Jean-Baptiste Thibault. Another priest, Albert Lacombe, founded Saint Albert, a home for Métis—people of mixed white and Native descent—near present-day Edmonton in 1861. The missionaries helped establish communities in the wilderness of the west and founded Alberta's first schools and agricultural colonies.

Mounties and Railroads

While Prince Rupert's Land was being mapped and settled, the colonies of eastern Canada were establishing themselves as the independent nation of Canada, a confederation of provinces. The Dominion of Canada was declared in 1867, and the new nation wished to exploit the resource-rich western lands. In 1869, the Canadian government purchased Prince Rupert's Land from the Hudson's Bay Company; this purchase more than doubled the size of Canada. The newly purchased region was reorganized as the North West Territories.

In addition to wanting to exploit the territories' natural resources, the Canadian government had another reason for acquiring western Canada: It feared an invasion by the United States. Traders and speculators from the south had long been making forays into British North America. As its western lands were being settled, the United States was growing stronger militarily and economically, and the emerging Canadian nation was afraid that this aggressive neighbor might try to swallow up the Canadian west. Alberta was especially vulnerable, because traders from Montana and other western states had already set up forts there. They were trading cheap liquor to the Natives, who were unaccustomed to alcohol and quickly became addicted to it. With names like Fort Whoop-up, Fort Stand-off, and Fort Slide-out, these posts disrupted the peace of the prairies. The Canadian government was on the verge of losing control.

In 1875, the North West Mounted Police—better known as the Mounties—brought law enforcement into the territory that is now Alberta.

To the rescue came a new law enforcement organization: the Mounties. The North West Mounted Police (or NWMP, now called the Royal Canadian Mounted Police, or RCMP) were clad in bright red uniforms and assigned to protect Canada's interests in the North West Territories. They arrived in Alberta in 1875 and promptly warned off the whiskey traders. They established a permanent post in southern Alberta, naming it Fort Macleod after its commander, James F. Macleod.

The NWMP soon established close relationships with various Native groups. Relations between the troops and the Natives were so cordial at first that the Mounties convinced the Natives to sign a number of treaties with the Canadian government. Agreements with the Cree in central Alberta, the Blackfoot and Blood in the south, and the Beaver and Woodland Cree in the north won huge tracts of land for the government. The Natives were removed from their ancestral lands and forced to live on reserves, where most of their descendants—many of whom are now disputing the treaties with lawsuits—live today.

The Mounties established law and order, but settlement of Alberta remained slow. Things picked up slightly after 1878, when the NWMP set up a second fort in the south. They called it Calgary. Located on the Bow River, Calgary attracted a population of Mounties, grain farmers, and cattle ranchers. Another population center grew up around Fort Edmonton, on the North Saskatchewan River. Edmonton was originally the headquarters of the western fur trade, but later expanded its economic base to include a sawmill and other businesses to serve the shipping traffic on the river. Canada was eager to connect the developing west—with valuable resources of timber, minerals, grain, and livestock—to the eastern provinces. The central government had promised to build a railway link between British Columbia and Ontario by 1885, and that promise spurred the construction of the Canadian Pacific Railway (CPR) across Canada's 3,000 miles (4,800 kilometers).

The railroads brought a new era of change and growth to western Canada. Here, the first train to cross the North Saskatchewan River enters Edmonton.

ALBERTA WOMEN ATTENDING PARLIAME
OF EQUAL SUFFRAGE BILL — EDMON

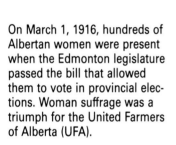

On March 1, 1916, hundreds of Albertan women were present when the Edmonton legislature passed the bill that allowed them to vote in provincial elections. Woman suffrage was a triumph for the United Farmers of Alberta (UFA).

To the dismay of the people of Edmonton, a southerly route via Calgary was chosen for the railway line through Alberta. By 1891, however, a spur line had brought Edmonton into the railway network. As years passed, more railroads and highways were built, forming a transportation web across the prairies. Nevertheless, the population remained small. A decade after the arrival of the railroad, only about 17,500 people lived in what is now Alberta. But the first of several western population booms occurred during the late 1890s. Good, affordable farmland was becoming scarce in eastern Canada and the United States, and many settlers eagerly accepted the chance to homestead in Alberta. When a new strain of fast-growing wheat was developed for Alberta's short growing season, thousands of farmers arrived to work the rich soil of the region. By 1901, Alberta's population had risen to about 75,000.

URING PASSAGE
TA. MAR 1ST 1916

Edmonton had its own population explosion at the end of the 19th century, when gold was discovered in the Klondike region of the Yukon Territory. Wisely calling itself the Gateway to the North, Edmonton attracted hopeful prospectors who were making their way to the Klondike from all over North America. Many of them decided to stay in Edmonton rather than face the arduous 2,000-mile (3,200-kilometer) journey into the Yukon. They opened stores, hotels, and businesses in the town that eventually became the province's capital.

Alberta Comes Into Its Own

Although settlement was slow, the North West Territories finally became too crowded to manage under a single administration. Alberta was made an individual province in 1905. The name

VOTE FOR

THE
UNITED FARMERS' CANDIDATE
IN
BOW RIVER CONSTITUENCY

OPPOSED
TO
CLASS
LEGISLATION

EQUAL
RIGHTS
FOR ALL

E. J. GARLAND
RUMSEY, ALTA.

Issued by the Bow River Constituency, U.F.A. Association

| J. C. BUCKLEY | MRS. MARY PUNCKE | G. A. FORSTER | H. W. LEONARD |
| President | 1st Vice-President | 2nd Vice-President | Secretary |

A. R. Lutsbury, Printer, Calgary

This UFA campaign poster dates from 1921, the year the UFA won control of Alberta's government. The party remained in power in the province until 1935.

Alberta was chosen by the governor-general of Canada in honor of his wife, Princess Louise Caroline Alberta, one of the daughters of Queen Victoria of Great Britain. The people of Calgary expected their city to be the provincial capital, but to their chagrin Edmonton was chosen instead.

The agricultural boom continued. People arrived to work the land, raise cattle, and establish communities. By 1921, the province's population had reached 584,454. At the same time, the independent pioneer spirit of the ranchers and farmers carried over into provincial politics. Albertans, like the people of the other western provinces, felt that their interests were often passed over in favor of those of the wealthier and more powerful eastern provinces. Throughout the prairies, new political parties sprang up to combat what many perceived as neglect or mistreatment by the federal government.

One of the first and most enduring of these organizations was the United Farmers of Alberta (UFA). The UFA was established in 1909 and in turn created the Alberta Farmers Co-Operative Elevator Company, which later became part of the United Grain Growers. These collective associations of prairie farmers worked to win better earnings for the western farmers by fighting against eastern companies' grain-pricing policies. In 1915, the UFA organized the United Farm Women of Alberta to campaign for women's voting rights. The challenge was met: Albertan women were granted the right to vote in provincial elections in 1916. (All Canadian women gained the right to vote in federal elections in 1918.)

The increasingly popular UFA also worked toward providing better health care services and schools. In 1921, the UFA's political party came to power in the provincial elections, and it remained in power until 1935. The UFA was renamed the United Farmers of Alberta Co-Operative Ltd. in 1948, and it remains one of the strongest farmer-owned organizations in Alberta.

Alberta's boom times came to a crashing halt in 1929, the start of the worldwide Great Depression. Grain prices collapsed and the once-important coal-mining industry rapidly declined. To make matters worse, a long drought destroyed many prairie farms. For the first time in Alberta's history, its population dropped. Thousands of people left the barren plains hoping to find work elsewhere.

As economic conditions worsened, political agitation increased. In 1932, the UFA began to lose its power and a new brand of politics arose. William Aberhart, an Albertan evangelist who ran a popular religious radio program, became a champion of the political and economic ideas of a British military officer named C. H. Douglas. According to Douglas, the world's economic depression occurred simply because people did not have enough money to buy the goods and services that were available. He proposed that the government should set fair prices for all goods and should give a cash dividend—called a social credit—to all consumers, who could use the money to make purchases that would revitalize the economy. Aberhart founded the Social Credit party in 1934. The struggling, hungry people of Alberta liked his message, especially when he promised a dividend of $25 a month to everyone in the province. Aberhart and his fellow Social Creditors trounced the UFA in the 1935 elections, winning 56 of the 63 seats in the provincial legislature. But the most extreme Social Credit policies, such as the distribution of cash dividends, were never applied in Alberta. The federal government overturned some Social Credit plans, and the federal courts declared others unconstitutional. This only increased the Albertans' resentment of federal interference. Support for the Social Credit party remained strong, especially when the province began to emerge from the Great Depression. Many people felt that the Social Credit party had put Alberta back on its feet. The Social Creditors, with their strong antifederal policies, remained in control until 1971, when the Conservative party took power.

Contemporary Issues

No event in Alberta's economic history matches the significance of the oil strike at Leduc, south of Edmonton, in February 1947. An energy-hungry North America was emerging from World War II. With manufacturing power at an all-time high, fuel was needed for factories throughout the western hemisphere and for an increasing number of automobiles. By the end of 1947, the Leduc field boasted 23 oil-producing wells. In 1948, drilling revealed oil at Woodbend, west of Edmonton, and at Redwater, to the north of the capital. Oilmen swarmed into the province, dotting the prairie landscape with oil rigs and boosting the province's economy. New industries developed, transportation was improved, and pipelines were laid to carry Alberta's oil to markets in Canada and in the United States. The principal beneficiaries of the energy boom were the cities of Calgary and Edmonton. Edmonton grew into an industrial and oil-refining center, as well as the hub of services, communication, and transportation for development in the northern part of the province. Calgary, the urban heart of the agricultural south, became the province's business and financial center.

Since the 1940s, energy has been Alberta's main export. One energy reserve that has not yet been fully exploited is the tar sands—sometimes called oil sands—of the Lake Athabasca region, where this plant was built to study various ways of extracting oil from the sand.

In 1989, 4 representatives of the Cree peoples of western Canada ran 2,700 miles (4,300 kilometers) from Alberta to New York City to seek the return of a tribal relic from the American Museum of Natural History. Their run dramatized the efforts of many Native groups to reclaim their artifacts and keep their heritage alive.

After the Middle Eastern oil-producing countries reduced their output of oil and raised oil prices in 1973, Alberta expanded its energy markets and experienced even greater prosperity. Income from oil and gas leases gave the provincial government an abundance of money to spend on social services. But during the 1980s, the province and the federal government came into conflict over the control of Alberta's natural resources. The federal government's National Energy Program, which had been designed to make Canada self-sufficient in energy production and to increase the federal share of income from oil, was met by an angry outcry from Alberta. In protest, Alberta decreased its oil production dramatically, forcing the federal government to import more oil from foreign countries. This crisis was resolved within months, but ill feelings persist between Ottawa, the federal capital, and Edmonton.

By 1990, a new dispute between the federal and provincial governments had arisen. This time the argument concerned Alberta's trees. After nearly a decade of lower oil and gas prices, the province's economic growth had slowed, and the provincial government looked to forestry to stimulate the sagging economy. One very controversial plan involves selling a tract of land as large as the state of Kansas to a Japanese company that would harvest the timber. The federal government insists that comprehensive studies of the effect of such large-scale logging on the environment must be done before the sale proceeds. Many Albertans, however, feel that Ottawa's interest in the forests is not environmental but economic, and that the Canadian government is using the conservation argument as a way of gaining control over the province's profitable forestry business.

Members of Alberta's growing environmental and conservation movement, however, are fighting the plans to harvest the forests. The environmentalists are worried about the loss of wildlife habitats and about the possible pollution of the province's air and water from the logging operations. Many Native American groups are also opposed to the growing forest industry; they claim that the land, and the trees that grow upon it, rightfully belongs to them—or at least that they should be part of the decision-making process. Both environmental concerns and the question of Native rights are certain to be important themes in Albertan politics throughout the 1990s and beyond. It is likely that the tug-of-war between the province and the federal government over control of provincial resources will also continue.

The Economy

Alberta's natural resources, including some of the most productive farmland in Canada as well as three-fifths of the country's mineral wealth, provided the province with a foundation upon which to build a dynamic economy, which flourished during the mid-20th century. The expansion of the oil industry after World War II shifted Canada's economic power to the west and increased Alberta's political and economic status in the country. The province's economic growth encouraged population growth by attracting young and vigorous newcomers, especially to the cities, where the service and financial industries were thriving.

Unfortunately, Alberta's economic health is at the mercy of external factors. The prices of oil and grain—Alberta's principal export products—can easily shift up and down as the world market for these commodities changes. Both markets boomed during the 1970s and then suffered serious declines during the 1980s, bringing an economic recession to the province and to Canada as a whole. With its continued supply of natural resources and a determined, self-reliant population, however, Alberta may well regain its economic vigor and its political prominence in the 1990s and beyond.

Opposite: Oil pumps dot the plains near the city of Leduc. The oil strike here in 1947 made Alberta an economic and political power among the provinces of Canada.
Above: The Calgary Airport is one of many sites where construction took place during the oil boom.

Agriculture

An early European settler, Captain John Palliser, reported in 1858 that Alberta consisted of "semi-arid desert unfit for farming." But hardworking settlers created irrigation systems to make up for the lack of adequate rainfall and even developed a strain of fast-growing wheat to compensate for the region's relatively short growing season. As a result, Alberta's present-day agricultural industry is of major importance to the province and to Canada. Alberta is Canada's largest producer of barley and oats and its second largest producer of wheat (after Saskatchewan).

About 50 million acres (20 million hectares) of the province's area are considered suitable for farming. Half of that land is currently being cultivated. Cereal crops, specifically wheat and barley, earn approximately $1.75 billion each year. Other specialty crops, such as sugar beets, corn, and alfalfa, are also grown, adding another $350 million. But nearly half of Alberta's total agricultural earnings comes from cattle ranching. Since 1877, when a settler from Montana brought 14 cows, 10 calves, and a bull to Fort Macleod, Alberta has raised some of the finest cattle in North America. The livestock industry is centered in the southeastern part of the province and in the foothills of the Rockies. Livestock sales total about $1.8 billion annually. Dairying and sheep farming are also important sources of income for the province.

Mining and Energy

Alberta's mineral resources are vital to its economy and its power within the Canadian confederation. In 1985, experts estimated that the value of Alberta's mineral resources—including oil, gas, and coal—amounts to 61 percent of the value of Canada's total mineral reserves.

The province's fossil fuels are the mainstay of its mining industry. Coal was mined first at Lethbridge, in 1872, and later at Drumheller, on the Red Deer River. By the 1980s, coal mines had been excavated on the prairies, in the foothills, and in the mountains. Most of the excavation sites are open pits that are mined from the surface, although underground mining is common in the mountains. Alberta's mines yield 25 to 30 million tons of coal each year.

The first oil well in the province was sunk at Turner Valley, just outside of Calgary, in 1914. But it was not until 1947, with the great oil strike at Leduc, that the oil boom in Alberta began in earnest. By 1990, more than 17,000 oil wells were operating throughout the province, yielding more than 88 percent of the petroleum produced in Canada. About 25 percent of this oil is used in Alberta, another 25 percent is exported to the United States, and 50 percent is used by other Canadian provinces.

While exploring for oil, miners discovered another valuable resource—natural gas. First located near Medicine Hat in 1883, natural gas was originally burned off as waste or used as an inexpensive energy source within the province. But natural gas is easier than oil to extract from the earth, and it is more abundant than oil in Alberta. Its value has been widely recognized, and it is now refined to produce butane and propane. Pipelines carry the gas to eastern Canada, to British Columbia, and to the United States. Alberta produces approximately 88 percent of Canada's natural gas—enough to fuel about 25 percent of the country's overall energy needs.

Not only does Alberta have large reserves of coal, oil, and natural gas, but it also contains some of the largest quantities of tar sands in the world. In the Athabasca River valley, more than 8,800 square miles (23,000 square kilometers) of sand is covered with a sticky, oillike substance called bitumen. After it is separated from the sand—by a complicated process that requires special refineries—bitumen can be processed into crude oil. Since the 1960s, when oil prices began to rise, much attention has been focused on Alberta's tar sands. A plant has been built at Fort McMurray in the northeast to extract and process the bitumen. Some energy experts claim that the Athabasca tar sands could provide fuel for Canada and the rest of the world for centuries.

In addition to its fossil fuels, Alberta also has the world's largest store of elemental sulphur, which is used in making gun-

Bales of hay provide winter feed for livestock in southwestern Alberta. Ranching, dairying, and wheat growing are the bastions of Albertan agriculture.

powder and matches. Small amounts of gold, iron ore, and uranium are also mined in the province.

Manufacturing and Industry

The province's largest manufacturing sector involves the processing of agricultural products, particularly beef. Most of the meat-packing plants are located in Calgary or Edmonton. Taber, a small city near Lethbridge in the south, is another important food-processing center, with a sugar refinery for locally grown sugar beets and other factories that package peas, corn, and various crops. Flour mills operate in Lethbridge and Medicine Hat, and dairies are scattered throughout the province.

During the 1970s and early 1980s, the oil boom led to a surge in the construction industry. Edmonton and Calgary, Canada's fastest-growing cities, were the centers of commercial and residential construction during this period. When oil prices declined in the mid-1980s, the construction industry suffered as

A climber on Mt. Edith Cavell in Jasper National Park is surrounded by a sea of Rocky Mountain peaks. Magnificent scenery and a wide range of outdoor activities draw more tourists to Alberta each year.

well. By the late 1980s, the total value of construction work in Alberta was $10 billion to $12 billion a year—a drop of about 12 percent since 1983.

Tourism earns the province almost $2 billion every year. Nearly 75,000 people are employed full-time in the tourist industry. Many of these people work in the province's parks; Alberta has more national and provincial parks than any other province. The Banff and Jasper national parks in the Rocky Mountains are the most popular, but the Peace River valley, the badlands, and the hunting and fishing areas of the forested northeast draw tourists as well. Alberta's major cities, Calgary and Edmonton, boast both indoor and outdoor attractions, including fine symphony orchestras, museums, sports events, dance and theater companies, and many historic sites located in lush green parks.

Forestry

More than half of Alberta is forested, and forestry is a potentially huge and profitable industry. As of 1990, however, only a small fraction of this potential was being realized, and the income from forest industries, including lumber and wood-pulp mills, was only $60 to $70 million a year. The development of Alberta's forests is a controversial topic, on both environmental and political grounds. Some Albertans believe that the province needs to fully exploit its forest resources in order to bolster a sagging economy—even, if necessary, by selling huge tracts of land to foreign investors. But other citizens indicate that some of the nations who want to buy up Alberta's forests have poor environmental records; Japan is the prime example. Opponents to these projects feel that unrestrained exploitation may cause serious environmental problems and provide only short-term economic benefits. At the beginning of the 1990s, the future of the forests was one of the most pressing issues facing the people of Alberta.

The People

Between 1901 and 1911, the first of Alberta's two major population spurts took place. Thousands of immigrants came in search of open land to farm. Many of these newcomers were from Germany, the Ukraine (a region in what is now the western part of the Soviet Union), Norway, Sweden, Denmark, and France. They brought with them their traditional religions, ways of life, and customs, giving Alberta a rich ethnic and cultural blend. During the oil boom of the 1970s, Alberta experienced its second great wave of immigration. Between July 1973 and July 1984, the population increased from 1,768,500 to 2,367,400. This time, most of the newcomers came from other parts of Canada and from the United States.

Calgary and Edmonton, the largest cities, are ethnic mosaics, with people of many cultures and backgrounds living side by side. Other parts of the province are more homogenous—that is, the populations in some areas tend to be made up mostly of people with a common ethnic background. For instance, people of Ukrainian descent account for six percent of Alberta's population,

Opposite: Banff Indian Days is one of many events that feature Native American dances, crafts, and exhibits. Natives make up about 2.5 percent of the province's population, and most of them live on reserves. *Above:* Tourists in Jasper pass a Lutheran church. Many such churches were built by the German and Scandinavian immigrants who settled in Alberta in the early years of the 20th century.

and most of them live in the Peace River valley. Many communities in this grain-farming district have a distinctly Ukrainian flavor, with Russian-style onion-domed churches and traditional foods, names, and holidays. Another center of Ukrainian settlement may be found east of Edmonton. Lethbridge is the home of a dynamic Japanese community that developed when many Japanese-Canadian families settled there after they were forced to move from British Columbia during World War II.

Native Americans, most of whom live in reserves that are scattered across the province, make up about 2.5 percent of the population. Although the Natives have long been denied access to economic and political power in Alberta (as elsewhere in Canada), many tribal groups and Native rights organizations are now waging lawsuits against the government in the hope of regaining land that they feel was wrongfully taken from them. The Cree Lubicon, for example, have been locked in a battle with the government over oil-rich territory in northern Alberta. The government wants to allow companies to drill for oil, whereas the Cree contend that the land is sacred ground that was illegally taken from their tribe. Similar claims are likely to be hotly contested throughout the 1990s and beyond. As in other parts of Canada, the Native peoples of Alberta are struggling to maintain their culture and to increase their political and economic power.

As of 1990, more than half of Alberta's inhabitants live in either Calgary or Edmonton. Another 10 percent live and work on farms. The rest of the population lives either in smaller cities, such as Lethbridge and Red Deer, or in the small rural towns that dot the province, especially in its southern half. As is true throughout Canada, population is greatest in the south. But whether they are urban denizens or small-town folk, Albertans as a group possess an independent pioneer spirit and are proud of their province's magnificent landscapes and natural bounty.

Education and Culture

For a long time Alberta and the other western provinces were regarded as unsophisticated rural outposts—far from Toronto,

Children of Korean descent take part in the ethnic festival of Heritage Days. Alberta's Asian-Canadian population also includes sizable Japanese and Chinese communities.

Montreal, and the other urban centers of eastern Canada—but that image is outdated. Alberta not only has two of Canada's liveliest big cities but offers its residents a wealth of educational and cultural opportunities.

More than 450,000 young Albertans attend grades 1 through 12 every year. Some of Alberta's schools are affiliated with either the Roman Catholic church or Protestant religious denominations. These private institutions are called separate schools. The Alberta Early Childhood Services program operates preschools for toddlers throughout the province.

Four universities, all liberal arts institutions with both graduate and undergraduate programs, educate some 50,000 students annually. The University of Calgary and the University of Lethbridge are the centers of learning in their respective cities.

Athabasca University is a correspondence college in which students take classes by receiving texts and tapes through the mail. The University of Alberta, founded in 1908 in Edmonton, is one of the largest schools in western Canada. It has more than 20,000 students and offers programs in medicine, law, business, and education. But one of this university's most impressive programs takes place deep in the Rocky Mountains. The Banff School of Fine Arts opened in 1933 and is one of the world's leading centers for the study of theater, painting, and music.

Many graduates of the Banff School of Fine Arts are able to find work in Alberta, especially in Calgary and Edmonton. Painting thrives in Calgary, which has more art galleries relative to its population than any other community in Canada. Among the important painters of Alberta's landscape are W. J. Phillips, W. L. Stevenson, and Illingsworth Kerr. In the 1960s and 1970s, a group of painters who were associated with the Edmonton Art Gallery introduced the style known as abstract expressionism to Alberta. With support from the government's Alberta Art Foundation, new artists continue to create and display their work in galleries and museums across the province.

Calgary may dominate Alberta's art scene, but Edmonton is western Canada's performing arts center. It has more theater companies than any other city its size in Canada. The Edmonton Symphony and the Edmonton Opera Association are internationally known for their fine performances. The Alberta Ballet, also based in Edmonton, is Canada's only professional ballet company west of Winnipeg, Manitoba. The Alberta Contemporary Dance Theatre specializes in works by modern choreographers.

Calgary also has a variety of performing arts organizations. The newly constructed Calgary Centre for the Performing Arts is home to the Calgary Philharmonic Orchestra and Theatre Calgary, a professional theater group. Working to bring new plays to the stage is Alberta Theatre Projects, an organization that encourages local writers to create experimental and avant-garde plays.

Many renowned writers of both nonfiction and fiction are based in Alberta. Regional historians, including Hugh Dempsey and James MacGregor, chronicle prairie life and Alberta's rich history. Robert Kroetsch, W. O. Mitchell, and Rudy Wiebe are novelists whose works are concerned with various aspects of modern life in Alberta. The University of Calgary library has one of the country's most extensive collections of Canadian writers' papers.

Impressive museums in cities and towns across the province display everything from fine arts and sculpture to plants and animals, fossils and historic artifacts. The Glenbow Museum in Calgary houses a large collection of Native American arts and crafts. The gallery of the Alberta College of Art, also in Calgary, displays the works of local and international artists. The Muttart Conservatory in Edmonton is an architectural masterpiece: Four massive glass pyramids contain plants from around the world, each in a meticulously re-created natural habitat. The Provincial Museum and Archives of Alberta in Edmonton is a center for research and study of the province's history.

History buffs and tourists alike can enjoy the province's various festivals and living museums. Fort Macleod Museum depicts the life of the Mounties during the 19th century. Heritage Park, located a few miles from Calgary, is a 66-acre (26.7-hectare) replica of a pioneer town. The province's biggest historical celebration, however, is a 10-day festival held annually in Edmonton. It is called Klondike Days, and it re-creates the rowdy excitement of the gold rush with parades, parties, and even some speculative panning for gold. Local residents as well as visitors dress in old-fashioned clothing, pretending to be prospectors, dance-hall girls, and other colorful figures from the Klondike era.

Some of Alberta's most important historical attractions date from the age of dinosaurs, millions of years ago. Many superb fossils have been found in Alberta, especially in the badlands along the Red Deer River, an area that eons ago was a humid, subtropical swamp in which many forms of ancient life flourished. The Tyrrell Museum of Paleontology, the Drumheller Prehistoric Park, and Dinosaur Provincial Park preserve these relics and display them to the public. More than just museums, however, these are among the world's prime paleontological sites,

Dinosaurs were some of the province's earliest inhabitants. Several museums are showcases for reconstructions and fossil exhibits. The fossil fields of Alberta are among the richest in the world.

Rodeo is the favorite sport of most Albertans, and the Calgary Stampede—held every summer—is one of the biggest rodeos in North America.

where scientists continue to uncover secrets of the past that have been buried in the earth for millions of years. Dinosaur Provincial Park contains one of the most extensive fields of dinosaur relics in the world and has been named a United Nations World Heritage Site.

Sports and Recreation

Alberta has more national and provincial parks than any other province. As a result, Albertans in general have a great love of the outdoors. The lure of outdoor recreation also draws many of the province's visitors. Among the most popular activities are skiing in the Rockies, especially at Banff and Jasper; hiking and camping in the Rockies; hunting and camping in Wood Buffalo National Park; and fishing for trout in the Bow River. Horseback riding, golf, and tennis are also popular. Albertans have created indoor recreation parks so that they can enjoy swimming, ball games, and even bodysurfing during the province's long, cold winters. Both Calgary and Edmonton have several of these leisure centers.

Alberta has two of the top teams in the National Hockey League, the Calgary Flames and the Edmonton Oilers. Both have won the Stanley Cup, hockey's most prestigious trophy. The Oilers attracted worldwide attention during the 1980s when hockey superstar Wayne Gretzky led the team to a series of championships. The Edmonton Brick Men represent that city in the Canadian Soccer League, and the Eskimos represent it in the Canadian Football League. Calgary's professional football team is the Calgary Stampeders.

But the most popular spectator sport in Alberta is the rodeo. Some 50 professional rodeos are held in Alberta every year. One of the biggest and best rodeos in North America is the Calgary Stampede, which takes place annually at the beginning of July. It is a 10-day spree of horsemanship, championship chuck-wagon racing, livestock shows, and nightly parties and concerts. Many Albertans feel that the Stampede symbolizes the spirit of their province: lively, powerful, lighthearted, and daring.

The Cities

Since Alberta's early settlement, Calgary and Edmonton have competed to become the province's most important city. Calgary won the first round when the Canadian Pacific Railway passed through Alberta at Calgary in the 1880s. Edmonton rebounded in 1905 when it was chosen as the provincial capital. Since that time, both cities have thrived, each becoming a leader in the arts, industry, and education. In the future they may be more closely connected than ever; plans are underway to build a high-speed train line between the two cities.

Edmonton has come a long way since its days as an isolated fur-trading post during the 19th century. It is strategically situated between the agriculturally productive south and the resource-rich north. In the early 1940s, Edmonton was a hub of activity during the construction of the Alaska Highway. Later it became a processing center for the petroleum industry. Now it is the heart of western Canada's oil-refining and petrochemical industries.

Opposite: Edmonton, the capital of Alberta, started out as a fur-trading post on the bank of the North Saskatchewan. In recent years, it has been one of Canada's fastest-growing cities, with a cosmopolitan urban culture as well as a dramatic skyline.
Above: Calgary's best-known symbol is the Saddledome, a sports arena with a saddle-shaped roof that was built for the 1988 Winter Olympics.

According to the 1986 census, 574,000 people live within the city's 260 square miles (680 square kilometers). For many years, Edmonton has been one of the two or three fastest-growing cities in Canada. Its population increased sevenfold between 1941 and 1983, and its boundaries have been extended many times to accommodate new businesses and the housing developments that have sprung up during periods of economic growth. Nevertheless, the city remains one of the most attractive in the country, primarily because of the establishment in 1950 of Canada's first city planning department. Nearly 15 percent of Edmonton's area is parkland, most of it located in a 25-mile (40-kilometer) strip along the banks of the North Saskatchewan River. Factories and refineries are concentrated on the outskirts of the city; planners hoped that this would keep the inner city beautiful and control pollution, and their hopes have been realized to some extent. Pollution, however, is a growing problem.

Gleaming new skyscrapers built during the oil boom of the 1970s have replaced most of the city's older buildings. Edmonton has one of the most striking skylines in Canada and features many examples of architectural innovation. A link to the past remains along Jasper Avenue, the core of the business and retail district, where a number of old buildings have been preserved. Two blocks from Jasper Avenue is Winston Churchill Square, a small park surrounded by the city hall, a library, the law courts, and the municipal art gallery. Edmonton Centre, a complex of stores and offices connected by tunnels, is located on Winston Churchill Square as well.

One of Edmonton's most unusual attractions is the West Edmonton Mall, the world's largest shopping mall, with a dozen department stores, more than 800 specialty stores, and Canada Fantasyland—an amusement park complete with water slides and submarine rides—all under one roof.

Although it is still fondly known as Cowtown, Calgary, too, has come a long way since its early settlement. Edmonton's rival city was first a whiskey trading post and then a North West Mounted Police post. Calgary was also the heart of cattle ranching in the west. Today, it is the financial hub of the prairie prov-

inces. More than 500 oil and gas exploration companies, 400
service and supply firms, and 300 energy-related consulting firms
have headquarters in this growing city. Strategically located on
major rail, highway, and air routes, Calgary is also an important
transportation center. Southern Alberta's rich harvests of wheat
and other agricultural products are transported via Calgary,
which is the center of the Canadian Pacific Railway's operations
in western Canada. The city also has one of the largest airports in
the country, featuring a $130-million terminal built in 1977.

With a population of more than 636,000, Calgary is the
largest city in Alberta and the fifth largest in Canada. About 85
percent of Calgary's population claims English as their first lan-
guage; this is the highest percentage of any large Canadian city.
Calgary's population grew rapidly during the oil boom, when
new buildings sprouted almost overnight and the city's skyline
seemed to change hourly. But the excitement waned during the
oil slump of the mid-1980s, and Calgary's population declined as

The West Edmonton Mall is a
shopper's paradise, with more
than 800 stores and dozens of
activities, all under one vast
roof.

Calgary's Chinatown was founded by Chinese immigrants who came to work on the railways in the late 19th century and stayed on to establish a thriving neighborhood of shops, restaurants, and other businesses. Traditional Chinese events draw crowds of residents and tourists alike.

many people left for other parts of Canada that seemed more promising, such as the coast of British Columbia. By 1990, however, Calgary was growing again. Current estimates predict that more than 1 million people will live in Calgary by the mid-1990s.

Set against the panoramic backdrop of the Rocky Mountains, Calgary is located at the intersection of the Bow and the Elbow rivers. Another smaller stream, Nose Creek, winds through the city as well. Forming small valleys and bluffs, these waterways add charm to Calgary's big-city landscape. The city's area is about 190 square miles (500 square kilometers). Although it is a bustling metropolis, Calgary also contains one of the largest urban parks in the world, the Fish Creek Provincial Park, which forms the city's southern border. Nature is close at hand even in the heart of the financial and shopping district. The Devonian Gardens, an indoor park with gardens and waterfalls, is part of a downtown office complex and can be reached by tunnel from many parts of the city. One of Calgary's major attractions is the Olympic Saddledome, a sports arena built to host the 1988 Winter Olympics. With a roof shaped like a huge saddle—in honor of Cowtown history—the Saddledome symbolizes Calgary's high-spirited sense of style.

A provincial park called Kananaskis Country is just 1 hour from downtown Calgary and consists of 1,641 square miles (4,250 square kilometers) of rolling foothills, mountain lakes, and rushing rivers. Golfing, fishing, cycling, and horseback riding are just a few of the activities available to Calgary residents and to tourists who visit Kananaskis Country.

The small mountain town of Banff is one of Canada's top tourist attractions, offering skiing in the winter, hiking in the summer, and impressive scenery all year round. Like Alberta itself, Banff combines a rugged pioneer spirit with contemporary sophistication.

Things to Do and See

• **Calgary Tower,** Calgary: A 626-foot (190-meter) structure in the center of Calgary offers a spectacular view spanning 75 miles (120 kilometers) in all directions.

• **Glenbow Museum,** Calgary: Native American art and historical artifacts from the early days of settlement in western Canada are displayed here, along with one of the most extensive weapon collections in the country. Sculptures, paintings, and prints by Native and international artists are featured.

• **Calgary Centennial Planetarium and Science Center,** Calgary: Featuring a special-effects star show, this center also has a first-class observatory, a weather station, and a display of vintage aircraft.

• **Fort Calgary,** Calgary: An interpretative center with a series of audiovisual displays gives visitors an insight into the early days of the North West Mounted Police.

• **Calgary Zoo and Historic Park,** Calgary: With 1,400 live exhibits, this is Canada's second largest zoo. It includes the 8.2-acre (3-hectare) Dinosaur Park, featuring 50 life-size replicas of dinosaurs. Fossil collections include authentic skeletons, bones, and other relics of prehistoric times.

A giant aluminum replica of a pysanka, or Ukrainian Easter egg, greets visitors to Heritage Park in Vegreville, east of Edmonton, where Ukrainian Canadians hold an annual festival.

• **Heritage Park,** Calgary: A replica of a pioneer town, containing many genuine buildings that have been moved here from their original locations.

• **Tyrrell Museum of Paleontology,** Drumheller: Contains more than 30 complete dinosaur skeletons and more than 800 fossil specimens, tracing 3 billion years of history. Trails lead into the badlands, where visitors can see fossils in their natural location and observe paleontologists at work.

• **Head-Smashed-In Buffalo Jump,** Fort Macleod: The largest and best-preserved buffalo jump in North America. A museum presents a dramatic audiovisual reenactment of the buffalo hunt.

• **West Edmonton Mall,** Edmonton: The largest shopping mall in the world, with more than 800 stores, 100 restaurants, 35 theaters, a National Hockey League regulation-size ice rink, a 5-acre (2-hectare) water park with 20 water slides, and an indoor lake with trained dolphins and submarine races.

• **Edmonton Space Science Center,** Edmonton: The largest planetarium in Canada, with hands-on exhibitions as well as an IMAX movie theater.

• **Muttart Conservatory,** Edmonton: Housed within four glass pyramids are displays of plants and animals from desert, tropical forest, and temperate regions.

• **Fort Edmonton Park,** Edmonton: A re-creation of one of the Hudson's Bay Company's major fur trading posts from the mid-1800s in the heart of Edmonton.

• **Ukrainian Museum of Canada,** Edmonton: A celebration of Ukrainian culture in Alberta through displays of costumes, Easter eggs, dolls, and tapestries.

• **Lake Louise,** west of Banff: Brilliant green hues sparkle in this Rocky Mountain lake, one of the most photographed views in Canada.

A skier tests the slopes in Banff National Park. Alberta's ski season lasts from November to June.

• **Columbia Icefield,** between Lake Louise and Jasper: More than 150 square miles (389 square kilometers) of glacial ice and snow formed over thousands of years.

• **Jasper Tramway,** Jasper: This tramway soars 8,084 feet (2,464 meters) up Whistler's Mountain to offer spectacular views of the Rocky Mountains and the town of Jasper.

• **Olympic Saddledome,** Calgary: Home of the National Hockey League's Calgary Flames, this stadium boasts a concrete roof in the shape of a giant saddle.

Festivals

Winter: Christmas is celebrated throughout the province in December, especially at the **Christmas Box Concert** in Calgary and at the **Singing Christmas Tree Fair** in Edmonton. **Winter carnivals,** complete with snowmobile races, parades, and ice sculpting, take place across Alberta. One of the most exciting is the **Lake Louise Winter Festival** held in Banff in December. Hundreds of competitors rev up their motors for the **North American International Snowmobile Races** at Wetaskiwin. In March, Edmonton sponsors the **Western Superrodeo,** complete with broncobusting and other events.

Spring: The **rodeo** season is in full gear in villages and towns throughout the province, including Camrose, Red Deer, Vermilion, and Drumheller. Equestrians from all over Canada and the United States meet at the **Calgary International Horse Show** in May. Edmonton hosts the **International Children's Festival,** featuring games, parades, and other activities that celebrate children of all cultures and countries.

A fairground lights up the night at one of Alberta's many outdoor exhibitions.

Summer: Cowboys and onlookers flock to more than two dozen **rodeos** that take place in June. Edmonton hosts the **Jazz City International Festival,** one of the finest music festivals in western Canada. Red Deer is the site of an **International Folk Festival,** bringing musicians and artisans from all over North America. July finds thousands of visitors flocking to the **Calgary Stampede,** the largest rodeo in Canada. Also in July, the town of Vegreville sponsors the **Ukrainian Festival** to celebrate the vibrant culture of the Ukrainian people. Edmonton's **Klondike Days** festival glorifies

Surefooted mountain goats live on the high, steep slopes of the Rockies.

the gold rush of 1898; thousands of tourists and residents dress in costumes, pan for gold, watch parades, and attend barbecues and other parties. In August, the **Fringe Theatre Event,** a showcase for local and regional performers, attracts tens of thousands of people to Edmonton to attend one of the largest annual festivals of this kind.

Fall: Fort McMurray hosts its annual **Blueberry Festival** in September, while Calgary features the **Spring Meadows Masters,** a major horse show. In October, Alberta's German-Canadian citizens celebrate **Oktoberfest** in towns and cities throughout the province, including Hinton, Medicine Hat, and Red Deer. One of the biggest events of the rodeo year is held in Edmonton during the **Canadian Finals Rodeo.** Edmonton also hosts the annual **Farmfair,** an agricultural exhibition attracting farmers from all over western Canada.

Summer transforms the mountain meadows into carpets of wildflowers. The Columbia Icefield, in the background, is one of the largest concentrations of ice south of the Arctic Circle.

Chronology

1754   Anthony Henday, an agent of the Hudson's Bay Company, enters Alberta.

1778   Peter Pond of the North West Company builds the first permanent white settlement.

1788   Fort Chipewyan is built on the shore of Lake Athabasca. Alexander Mackenzie uses the fort as the starting point for several historic expeditions.

1821   The Hudson's Bay Company absorbs the North West Company and controls all of northern and western Canada, which is called Prince Rupert's Land.

1867   The eastern provinces form the Dominion of Canada, an independent new nation.

1869   Canada buys Prince Rupert's Land from the Hudson's Bay Company.

1878   Calgary is founded by the Mounties.

1885   The Canadian Pacific Railway is completed.

1905   Alberta is made a province.

1909   The United Farmers of Alberta (UFA) is established.

1934   The Social Credit party is founded.

1947   Drillers strike oil at Leduc, near Edmonton.

1980s   The province and the federal government argue over control of oil resources and revenues.

1988   Calgary hosts the Winter Olympics.

1990   Intensive logging of some of Alberta's forests is considered.

Further Reading

Berton, Pierre. *The Impossible Railway: The Building of the Canadian Pacific.* Magnolia, MA: Peter Smith, 1984.

Breen, David H. *The Canadian Prairie West and the Ranching Frontier.* Toronto: University of Toronto Press, 1983.

Ewars, John C. *The Blackfeet: Raiders on the Northwestern Plains.* Norman: University of Oklahoma Press, 1985.

Holbrook, Sabra. *Canada's Kids.* New York: Atheneum, 1983.

Howard, James H. *The Canadian Sioux.* Lincoln: University of Nebraska Press, 1984.

Kroetsch, Robert. *Badlands.* New York: Beaufort Books, 1983.

Kurelek, William. *A Prairie Boy's Summer.* Boston: Houghton Mifflin, 1975.

Law, Kevin. *Canada.* New York: Chelsea House, 1990.

MacGregor, James C. *A History of Alberta.* Seattle: University of Washington Press, 1981.

McNaught, Kenneth. *The Penguin History of Canada.* New York: Penguin Books, 1988.

Macpherson, C. B. *Democracy in Alberta: Social Credit and the Party System.* Toronto: University of Toronto Press, 1953.

Malcolm, Andrew. *The Canadians.* New York: Random House, 1985.

Newman, Peter C. *Caesars of the Wilderness: The Story of the Hudson's Bay Company.* New York: Penguin Books, 1988.

Smith, P. J., ed. *The Prairie Provinces.* Toronto: University of Toronto Press, 1972.

Wansbrough, M. B. *Great Canadian Lives.* New York: Doubleday, 1986.

Index

ACKNOWLEDGMENTS

Alberta Tourism: pp. 9, 11, 12, 13, 15, 32, 35, 36, 38, 41, 43, 46, 47, 52, 55, 56, 58, 59; AP/Wide World Photos: pp. 29, 30; Diana Blume: p. 6; Glenbow Archives, Calgary, Alberta: pp. 16, 17, 19, 20, 22, 23, 24–25, 26; The Mach 2 Stock Exchange Ltd./H. M. Pattison Dauer: pp. 3, 5; The Mach 2 Stock Exchange Ltd./Patrick Landes: pp. 33, 44; The Mach 2 Stock Exchange Ltd./Bill Marsh: cover, p. 8; The Mach 2 Stock Exchange Ltd./Ole Tenold: pp. 39, 49, 50, 51; Debora Smith: p. 7

Suzanne LeVert has contributed several volumes to Chelsea House's LET'S DISCOVER CANADA series. She is the author of four previous books for young readers. One of these, *The Sakharov File*, biography of noted Russian physicist Andrei Sakharov, was selected as a Notable Book by the National Council for the Social Studies. Her other books include *AIDS: In Search of a Killer, The Doubleday Book of Famous Americans*, and *New York*. Ms. LeVert also has extensive experience as an editor, first in children's books at Simon & Schuster, then as associate editor at *Trialogue*, the magazine of the Trilateral Commission, and as senior editor at Save the Children, the international relief and development organization. She lives in Cambridge, Massachusetts.

George Sheppard, General Editor, is a lecturer on Canadian and American history at McMaster University in Hamilton, Ontario. Dr. Sheppard holds an honors B.A. and an M.A. in history from Laurentian University and earned his Ph.D. in Canadian history at McMaster. He has taught Canadian history at Nipissing University in North Bay. His research specialty is the War of 1812, and he has published articles in *Histoire sociale/Social History, Papers of the Bibliographical Society of Canada*, and *Ontario History*. Dr. Sheppard is a native of Timmins, Ontario.

Pierre Berton, Senior Consulting Editor, is the author of 34 books, including *The Mysterious North, Klondike, Great Canadians, The Last Spike, The Great Railway Illustrated, Hollywood's Canada, My Country: The Remarkable Past, The Wild Frontier, The Invasion of Canada, Why We Act Like Canadians, The Klondike Quest*, and *The Arctic Grail*. He has won three Governor General's Awards for creative nonfiction, two National Newspaper Awards, and two ACTRA "Nellies" for broadcasting. He is a Companion of the Order of Canada, a member of the Canadian News Hall of Fame, and holds 12 honorary degrees. Raised in the Yukon, Mr. Berton began his newspaper career in Vancouver. He then became managing editor of *McLean's*, Canada's largest magazine, and subsequently worked for the Canadian Broadcasting Network and the *Toronto Star*. He lives in Kleinburg, Ontario.